MINDSET MATTERS

Change Your Mind   *Change Your World*

WORKBOOK

Copyright © 2021 by Dave Martin

Published by AVAIL

All rights reserved. No portion of this book may be reproduced, stored in a retrieval system, or transmitted in any form or by any means—electronic, mechanical, photocopy, recording, scanning, or other—except for brief quotations in critical reviews or articles, without prior written permission of the author.

For foreign and subsidiary rights, contact the author.

Cover design Joe De Leon

ISBN: 978-1-954089-26-6   1 2 3 4 5 6 7 8 9 10

Printed in the United States of America

MINDSET MATTERS

Change Your Mind — *Change Your World*

WORKBOOK

DR. DAVE MARTIN

AVAIL

CONTENTS

Overview and Suggestions for Use 6

Module 1. The Biggest Problem in the World 10

Module 2. Courage, Cowardice, and Conformity 18

Module 3. The Power of Goals 26

Module 4. How Thoughts Become Reality 36

Module 5. Why Don't People Know About This? 44

Module 6. The Price of Success 52

Module 7. The Proof Is in the Pudding 60

Module 8. The Price of Success 68

OVERVIEW AND SUGGESTIONS FOR USE

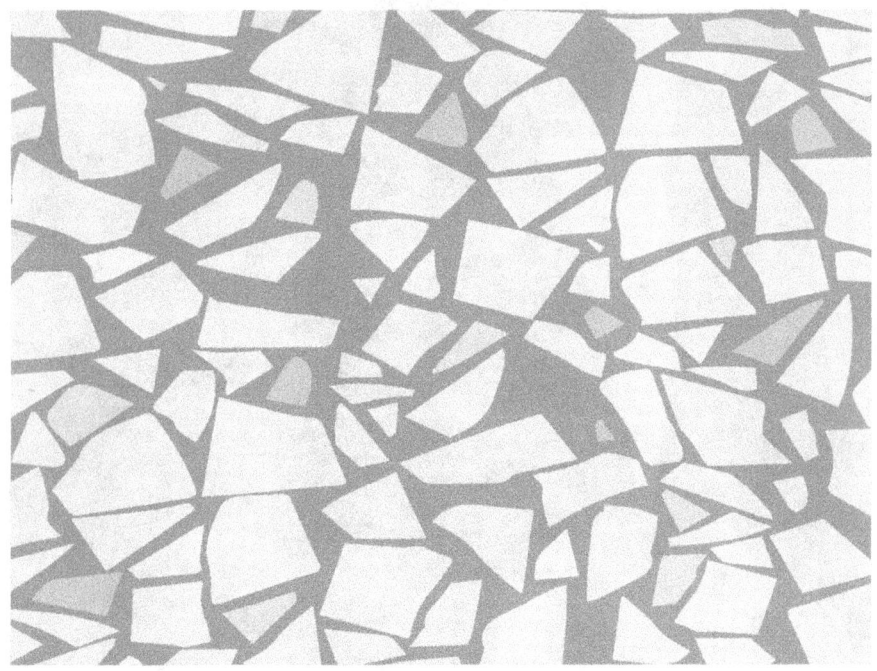

Welcome to our complementary workbook for *Mindset Matters: Change Your Mind, Change Your World*. Dave Martin International is proud to present you with our companion publication to Dr. Dave's powerful and thought-provoking book. This corresponding guide is the result of many hours of effort. Our hope is that you will make use of this helpful tool to learn more about the most basic—yet most neglected—ingredient for success in the modern world.

Before you start working your way through this helpful tool, however, please take some time to read through this *Overview and Suggestions for Use*. This brief prelude to our companion guide is designed to introduce you to the contents of the workbook's eight modules. After carefully reading the original book and this overview, you should then start at the beginning and work your way through the text of this supplemental guide in order to reinforce and retain the things you have learned.

The eight modules of this workbook correspond to the eight chapters of the book. Each module includes a series of questions that is designed to stimulate your thinking and to help you relate the material to your everyday life. Each module also includes a section where you can journal your thoughts and feelings as you come to understand the power of personal vision and the things that flow from it.

EACH MODULE CONTAINS…

- **Nuggets of Knowledge**—relevant quotations from some of the world's most successful and accomplished people. While Dr. Dave has a lot to share on the subject of vision and while he has learned much about success from his own personal experiences and his associations with others, he is not the first to convey the importance of focus in a person's life. These applicable gems of wisdom can aid you in seeing the subject matter of the book from different perspectives and help you encapsulate profound concepts and truths.

- **Summing Up**—memorable quotes by Dave Martin. To help you retain the key points that summarize his teachings, Dr. Dave offers these tidbits of wisdom.

- **Hands On** – creative activities designed to give you an even broader understanding of the power of personal vision and how you can experience that power in your own life. This section will help you practically apply the lessons learned from the book.

- **Snippets** – a summary of each chapter. Trusting these morsels of wisdom to memory will help you recall the primary lesson of each chapter you have read.

At the end of each chapter, you will find a place to record your perceptions and reactions, as well as any personal insights you may have received from the material. These entries could be very valuable to you in the future, so you should definitely take the time to record them.

WE SUGGEST YOU…

- Read each chapter in Dave Martin's book, *Mindset Matters: Change Your Mind, Change Your World*, before tackling the corresponding module in the workbook.

- Pace yourself to complete one chapter of the workbook each week. The material is designed for groups that would like to pursue a 40-day emphasis on the subject of personal success. But you may also use this workbook privately, and you don't have to adhere to a strict 40-day schedule. If you like, you can utilize the

material each day during your devotional time, or you can set aside a specific time each week to complete an entire chapter in one sitting. Whatever works for you, works for us.

- Be consistent in your study. Once you have established a time to complete your assignment, stick with it. Once you have established a place to do the work, be there. If you fall behind or unforeseen circumstances interrupt your plans, don't quit. Get back on track and push through, even if the process takes longer than you expected. You cannot reap the benefits of this compelling material without putting some effort into understanding it. So determine that you will faithfully invest the time and energy needed to absorb the life-changing truths contained in these two publications.

- Be honest with yourself as you answer each question. Combining the objective truths presented in the book with your own subjective insights can produce profound inspiration that is impossible to create any other way.

Too many people buy books impulsively, and then they put those books in a box or on a shelf and leave them there for years. But information that is not utilized is information that is worthless. For this reason, we are glad you have decided to invest the necessary time to learn about the primary key to success and to apply the truths you learn in a practical way. We join Dr. Dave Martin in wishing you the very best as you seek the benefits that can be derived from a directed life that is driven by an inward vision.

MODULE 1

THE BIGGEST PROBLEM IN THE WORLD

The biggest problem in the world today is that people lack any type of personal vision for their lives.

Please refer to Chapter 1 in Dr. Dave Martin's book,
Mindset Matters: Change Your Mind, Change Your World

In your opinion, what is the biggest problem in the world today? If you disagree with Dave Martin, explain why.

_____
_____
_____
_____
_____
_____

How has your environment (home life and culture) shaped your personal expectations of life?

_____
_____
_____
_____
_____
_____

How is an individual's lack of purpose and direction the root cause of most of the problems in his or her life?

_____
_____
_____
_____
_____
_____

Have you ever struggled with self-destructive behaviors or attitudes? If so, how did a lack of direction in your life contribute to this struggle?

_____
_____
_____
_____
_____

Of the people you know, what percentage would you say have a clear and driving motivation for their lives? How can you tell that a particular individual has an internal purpose that motivates him or her?

_____
_____
_____
_____
_____

When you were a child, what did you want to be when you grew up? What were your childhood expectations of a successful and fulfilling life?

_____
_____
_____
_____
_____
_____

NUGGETS OF KNOWLEDGE

The most pathetic person in the world is someone who has sight but no vision.
—Helen Keller

Live your vision and demand your success.
—Steve Maraboli

Throughout the centuries there were men who took first steps down new roads, armed with nothing but their own vision.
—Ayn Rand

As you grew beyond childhood into adulthood, did your expectations of life grow or diminish? Did you achieve your childhood dreams or abandon them? Why?

_____
_____
_____
_____
_____
_____

How do people suffer spiritually and psychologically due to the absence of a vision for their lives?

_____
_____
_____
_____
_____
_____

How do the rest of us suffer due to the absence of personal vision in people's lives?

_____
_____
_____
_____

What does "success" mean to you today? When you picture yourself living the last years of a highly successful life, what do you see as your life's achievements?

_____
_____
_____
_____
_____
_____

SUMMING UP

- People who do bad things to themselves and others are people who are dissatisfied with their lives or bitter toward a world that they believe has deprived them of their due rewards.

- A person whose hopes and dreams are dashed because he fails to meet any of his goals will soon give up on himself.

- The greatest problem we have in our country today and in much of the industrialized world is the problem presented by the millions of people who have no direction for their lives.

HANDS ON

Dave Martin proposes that the absence of individual passion and purpose lies at the root of all social and human problems.

What problems do you believe would be less common in our society if children grew up with an increasingly evident purpose for their lives?

_____
_____
_____
_____
_____
_____

If the problems you listed above could be minimized by a cultural understanding of the importance of personal initiative, how would that change our society and our nation? How would that change our world?

_____
_____
_____
_____
_____
_____

In your opinion, why do most people lack a definable purpose for their lives?

_____
_____
_____
_____
_____
_____

SNIPPETS

The biggest problem in our world today is the fact that most people have no purpose for their lives.

THE FINAL WORD

It is not enough to be industrious; so are the ants. What are you industrious about?
—HENRY DAVID THOREAU

Life is like a candle that is burning at both ends. Whether we like it or not, a little bit of our lives is consumed every day. So if our lives are going to be consumed anyway, we might as well make sure that our lives are consumed with something that is meaningful. After all, it is woven into the fabric of man's being to have purpose and legitimacy and to achieve significance and leave a legacy.

The people who do great things and leave a lasting mark upon the world are the people who have defined a purpose for the time they spend on this earth. They are the people who can "see" where their lives are headed and can see what they hope to achieve with their limited time. Since the candle is burning at both ends anyway, they are the people who make sure that their time and their talents and their treasures and their resources are being consumed in pursuit of something worthwhile and intentional. They refuse to let their lives become an "accident."

It is good to be busy. But to be fulfilled, a person must be busy with something that matters. He must be busy with something that counts and something that can fill all the empty places in his life. He must be busy with something that can positively impact others.

What is your vision for your life? Do you have one? If so, what is it? If not, why not? Search your heart and be honest with yourself. Know where you stand on this important aspect of life before you move forward into the next chapter of this book.

PERSONAL JOURNAL

Take a few moments to record your thoughts regarding this week's session on the world's biggest problem. What new things have you learned? What new insights have you received? What life-changing truths did Dr. Dave impart that have impacted you in a meaningful way?

MODULE 2

COURAGE, COWARDICE, AND CONFORMITY

Conformity is the most common expression of cowardice in the world today and the most certain pathway to failure.

Please refer to Chapter 2 in Dr. Dave Martin's book, *Mindset Matters: Change Your Mind, Change Your World.*

What does success mean to you?

_____
_____
_____
_____
_____

What does failure mean to you?

_____
_____
_____
_____
_____

Give an example from current events or everyday life that shows how conventional wisdom leads people to conform to nonproductive or dead-end behaviors.

_____
_____
_____
_____
_____
_____
_____
_____

Name a person, contemporary or historical, that you admire for his or her achievements. How was this person forced to resist the lure of conventional wisdom in order to achieve success?

___

What is something that you deliberately and persistently do in defiance of conventional wisdom because it brings you success in an important area of your life?

___

Give two or three examples from our popular culture of how conventional wisdom and "group think" lead people to do things they probably would not do if they were independent thinkers.

___

NUGGETS OF KNOWLEDGE

He who is not courageous enough to take risks will accomplish nothing in life.
—Muhammad Ali

The opposite of courage is not cowardice; it is conformity. Even a dead fish can go with the flow.
—Jim Hightower

Conformity is the jailer of freedom and the enemy of growth.
—John F. Kennedy

Do you regard yourself as a "victim" of any particular person, group, or circumstance? If so, how have you been victimized? How did you come to be victimized? What can you do to change your situation?

_____
_____
_____
_____
_____
_____

Why did you select your current profession? The community where you live? The key person in your life?

_____
_____
_____
_____

Do you find it easy or difficult to stand in opposition to your primary social community? Give an example.

_____
_____
_____
_____

Have your childhood dreams and goals died, or have they evolved into something more meaningful for you? Why did this happen? How did it happen?

_____
_____
_____
_____
_____
_____

SUMMING UP

- Success is the steady, gradual, and incremental achievement of a meaningful goal. It is the continual, relentless climb toward the vision that resonates within a person's heart.

- There is just something about human nature that makes us want to follow the herd, even when the herd is wandering around in circles or marching in unison over a cliff into the abyss below.

- If you want to be different, you have to think differently. You have to stop thinking like the ninety-six percent.

HANDS ON

On his march to significance, the person with a dream will encounter many obstacles, some of them human in form and some of them circumstantial. But according to Dave Martin, the biggest obstacle that a person will face in his journey to the top is the obstacle he creates for himself by his own limited thinking and the habits that flow from that thinking.

What are some of the "human" impediments you have encountered in your life as you have attempted to achieve your dreams and goals?

_____
_____
_____
_____
_____

What are some of the "circumstantial" impediments you have encountered in your life as you have attempted to achieve your dreams and goals?

_____
_____
_____
_____
_____

Name one or two problems in your own thinking that have caused you to miss opportunities in your life or to pursue less than noble goals.

_____
_____
_____
_____
_____

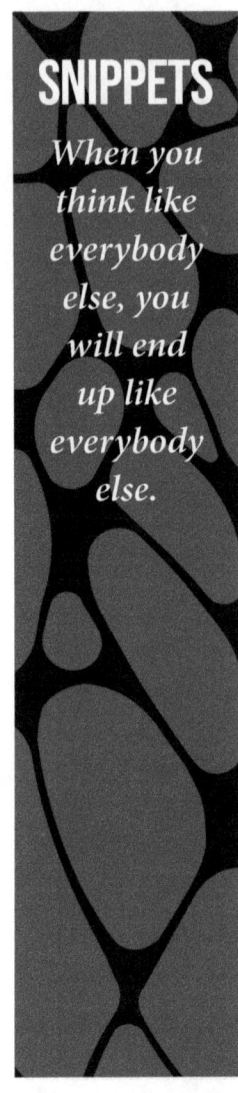

SNIPPETS

When you think like everybody else, you will end up like everybody else.

THE FINAL WORD

I think the reward for conformity is that everyone likes you except yourself.
—Rita Mae Brown

What has shaped you? What has molded your personality? What thoughts, ideals, and beliefs have crafted you into the person you have become? If you really think about it, you are being bombarded every waking moment of every day by external stimuli that can easily shape your thoughts, which can easily shape your life. But most of these stimuli go unnoticed.

When you were young, your parents obviously shaped your personality. But as you grew older, you discovered television and music and movies and books. When you became old enough to go to school, you were shaped further by your teachers, by your friends, and by all the things in the popular culture that you discovered through the new people in your life.

Each of these things had the power to "move" you and to cause you to develop your own distinct paradigm of life. You gradually became the expression of all the external influences that you embraced and that you allowed to govern your thinking. Now that you are older, however, you are more skeptical of these external stimuli. You are more skeptical of all the "voices" that want to influence you.

But these "voices" are so common, so persistent, and so familiar, they are difficult to recognize and hard to resist. To be successful, therefore, you must learn to recognize the art and the literature and the social patterns of thought that influence your own thinking. You must learn to "filter out" those things that are detrimental to you and to welcome those things that can help take you where you want to go in life. When necessary, you must learn to defy the crowd.

PERSONAL JOURNAL

Take a few moments to record your thoughts regarding this week's session on courage, cowardice, and conformity. What new things have you learned? What new insights have you received? What life-changing truths did Dr. Dave impart that have impacted you in a meaningful way?

MODULE 3

THE POWER OF GOALS

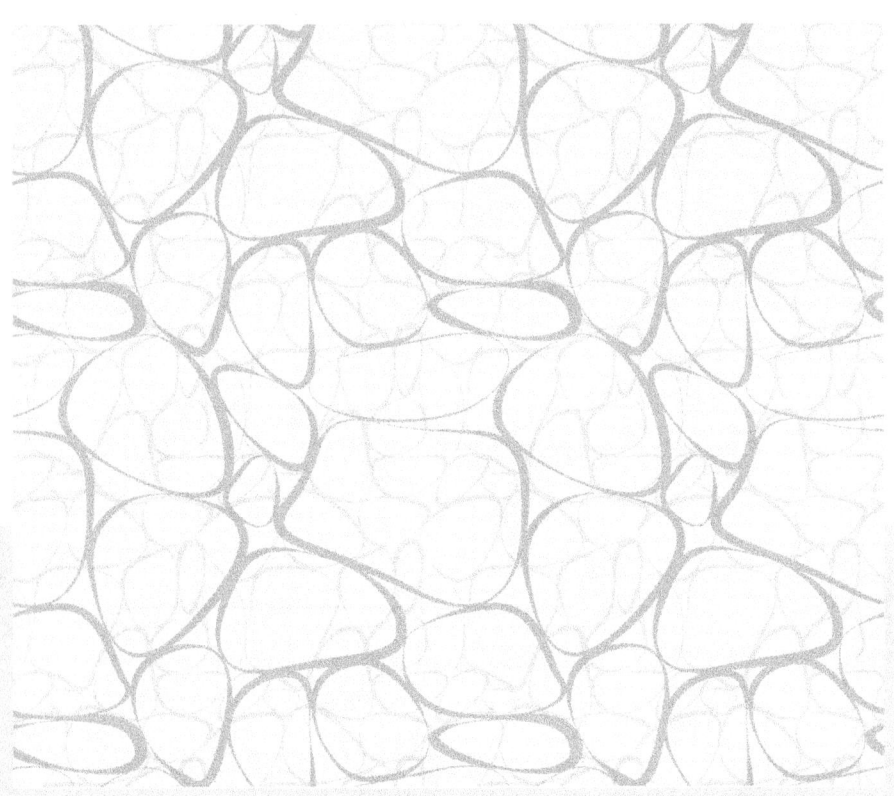

More than anything else, dreams and goals have the power to shape a person's destiny and to determine the outcome of a person's life.

Please refer to Chapter 3 in Dr. Dave Martin's book,
Mindset Matters: Change Your Mind, Change Your World.

When did you discover the concept of "vision" and its central role in the pursuit of success? Is this a new concept for you? If not, when were you first impacted by the idea of personal vision?

_____
_____
_____
_____
_____
_____

Can you think of a hard-working person you know who is not a success in your estimation or in his or her own estimation? Why is this person unsuccessful thus far in life?

_____
_____
_____
_____
_____
_____

Can you think of an intelligent person you know who is not successful by your standards or by his or her own standards? Why is this person unsuccessful at this point in life?

_____
_____
_____
_____
_____
_____

Why is it impossible for a person to achieve real and lasting success unless that person is consumed by something that is meaningful to him (or her) and that motivates him to walk a predetermined path to pursue it?

_____
_____
_____
_____

What would life be like if there were no forms of transportation with predetermined destinations? Use your imagination, and apply this scenario to the condition of people's lives.

_____
_____
_____
_____
_____
_____
_____
_____
_____

Do you concur with Dave Martin that most people have no aiming point, no destination for their lives? Why?

_____
_____
_____
_____
_____

> ## NUGGETS OF KNOWLEDGE
>
> *If you go to work on your goals, your goals will go to work on you. If you go to work on your plan, your plan will go to work on you. Whatever good things we build, end up building us.*
> —JIM ROHN
>
> *If you're bored with life—you don't get up every morning with a burning desire to do things—you don't have enough goals.*
> —LOU HOLTZ
>
> *If you set goals and go after them with all the determination you can muster, your gifts will take you places that will amaze you.*
> —LES BROWN

In your estimation, how can goals change the outcome of a person's life?

_____
_____
_____
_____
_____
_____

In your opinion, what did King Solomon mean when he wrote, "For as (a man) thinketh in his heart, so is he?"

_____
_____
_____
_____
_____
_____

In your opinion, what did Jesus mean when he said, "All things are possible to him who believes?"

_____
_____
_____
_____
_____
_____

How do a person's thoughts determine everything about that person's life and destiny?

_____
_____
_____
_____
_____
_____

SUMMING UP

- No person, no society, no human institution, and no government can guarantee success to the person who lacks vision for his own life.

- The person who thinks he can, can. And the person who thinks he can't, can't. The person who thinks she will, will. And the person who thinks she won't, won't.

- The outcome of one's life is linked not to outside forces, but to one's own internal thinking.

HANDS ON

According to Dave Martin, a journey on any form of public transportation is a lot like the journey through life. Trains, boats, buses, and airplanes have clearly defined destinations before they depart, and the crews of these vehicles are prepared for the trip ahead.

What similarities can you think of regarding the preparation of a vehicle for its departure and the preparation of an individual for his or her journey through life?

_____
_____
_____
_____
_____

What similarities can you think of regarding the mapping of the journey by a public vehicle and the mapping of a person's journey through life?

_____
_____
_____
_____
_____

What similarities can you think of regarding the movements and maneuvers of public vehicles carrying passengers to assigned destinations and individuals who are navigating the course of real life?

_____
_____
_____
_____
_____

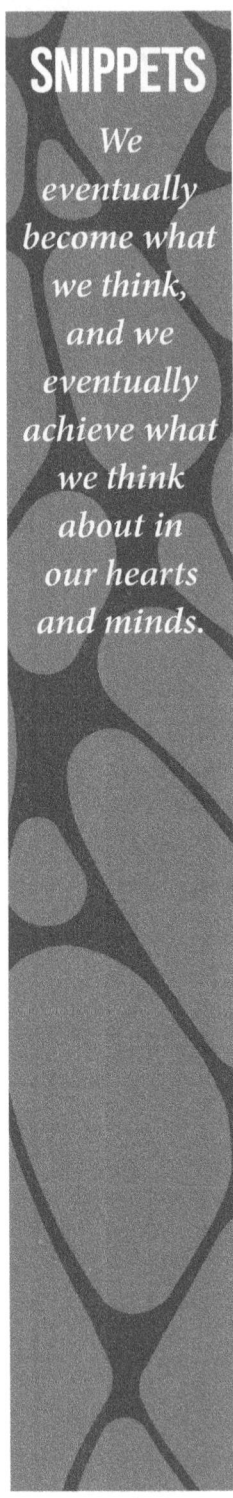

SNIPPETS

We eventually become what we think, and we eventually achieve what we think about in our hearts and minds.

THE FINAL WORD

What you get by achieving your goals is not as important as what you become by achieving your goals.
—HENRY DAVID THOREAU

We humans like to think that we are the product of our own efforts. And to a great extent, we are. But we also are the product of all the things that have been sown into us over the course of our lives.

When you were young, for instance, your parents shaped you in every way. They chose the information that you received, and they determined the values that shaped your early life. As you grew, you also were shaped by the culture that impacted your family environment. And when you became old enough to venture outside your house, you were influenced further by your friends, your teachers, and the popular culture in which you lived. It was not until you became older that you could actually think for yourself and differentiate between the forces that had shaped you earlier in your life and your own internal motivations toward a future that was uniquely your own.

Through every chapter of your life, however, it has been the joyful and victorious experiences that have taught you to be happy. And it has been the difficult experiences that have taught you resolve, fortitude, and patience. So your character has been forged over time by the thousands of small choices that you have made in the face of those things that have influenced you: choices to lie or to tell the truth, choices to be kind or to be cruel, choices to be generous or to be selfish.

But the things that have happened to you in the pursuit of your own unique set of passions are the experiences that have molded you into the person you have become, because the pursuit of any life goal is riddled with challenges, setbacks, defeats, victories, teamwork, isolation, and every other kind of experience that creates the fabric of one's life. So let your climb to success be a journey, not a jaunt. Let it be a marathon, not a sprint. When you finally achieve the goals you have established for yourself, the person you have become will be just as important as the things you have achieved because character is the most important byproduct of success.

PERSONAL JOURNAL

Take a few moments to record your thoughts regarding this week's session on goals and goal-setting. What new things have you learned? What new insights have you received? What life-changing truths did Dr. Dave impart that have impacted you in a meaningful way?

MODULE 4

HOW THOUGHTS BECOME REALITY

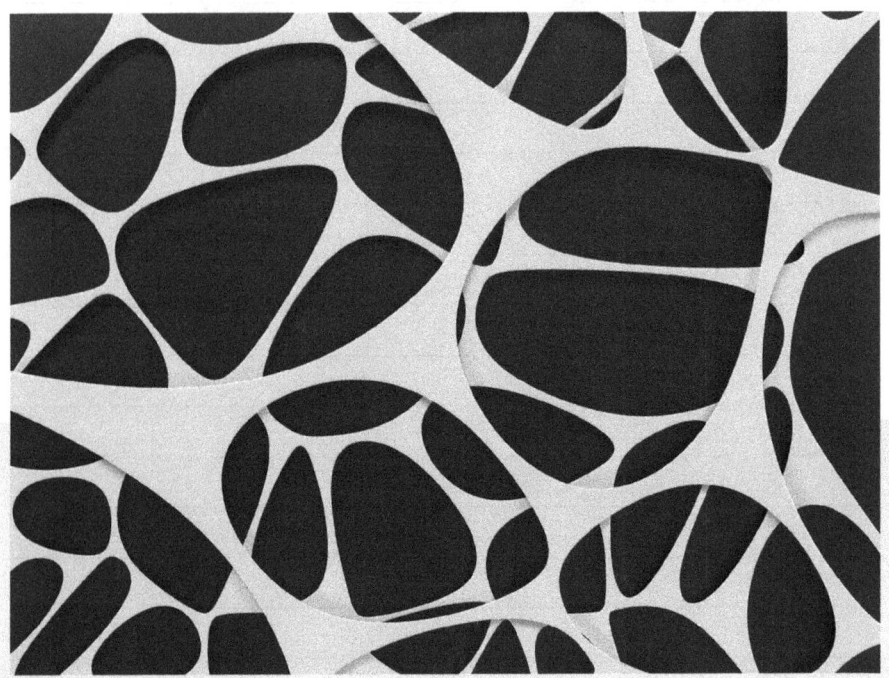

The thoughts we sow into our minds are the "seeds" that eventually produce a harvest in our lives, a harvest that will either be life-giving or destructive.

Please refer to Chapter 4 in Dr. Dave Martin's book,
Mindset Matters: Change Your Mind, Change Your World.

What was planted in your mind when you were young and impressionable? Do those things still affect your life today? How?

_____
_____
_____
_____
_____
_____

What good harvest (corn) have you seen in your life as a result of the things that were planted in your mind during your developmental years?

_____
_____
_____
_____
_____
_____

What destructive harvest (castor beans) have you seen in your life as a result of the things that were planted in your mind during your growing years?

_____
_____
_____
_____
_____
_____

Our minds don't care what kinds of seeds we sow in the soil of our own lives. Have your biggest decisions produced mostly success or failure? Mostly purpose or conformity? How?

_____
_____
_____
_____
_____
_____

What do you want to achieve in your life? What are your one or two primary goals?

_____
_____
_____
_____
_____
_____

Do you mostly spend your time around negative people or positive people? Do you mostly fill your mind with inspiring things or things that lead you nowhere? How has this shaped your life?

_____
_____
_____
_____
_____
_____

> ## NUGGETS OF KNOWLEDGE
>
> *My words, thoughts, and deeds have a boomerang effect.*
> —Allan Rufus
>
> *Once you shift your thoughts for the better, your world begins to shift with them..*
> —Marcey Shapiro
>
> *The human mind once stretched by a new idea never goes back to its original dimensions.*
> —Oliver Wendell Holmes

What are you "reaping" today in your life that is a direct result of the things you sowed into your own mind in the past?

_____
_____
_____
_____
_____
_____

Give one illustration of something positive and one illustration of something negative that our nation is "reaping" today as a result of the things our leaders thought about years ago.

_____
_____
_____
_____
_____
_____

What are you mostly thinking about at this point in your life? How will this shape your future?

_____
_____
_____
_____
_____

How can nuclear energy be bad for mankind? How can it be good? How does the analogy of nuclear energy pertain to our present thoughts and future consequences?

_____
_____
_____
_____
_____

SUMMING UP

- Our lives are the products of the deeds that we perform, the words that we speak, and the kinds of thinking that we allow to permeate our minds on a daily basis.

- The thoughts you sow into your mind are the thoughts that will eventually give rise to something tangible and lasting in your life.

- The things you reap in the future will be the consequence of the choices you make today. The outcome of tomorrow will be the direct result of the things you do right now.

HANDS ON

Any farmer understands the three laws of the harvest that govern the agricultural process. The farmer reaps what he sows, more than he sows, and after he sows the seeds into the ground.

What have you primarily sown into the fertile soil of your mind during your adult years? What would you prefer to sow into your mind from this point forward?

_____
_____
_____
_____

How have the seeds of thought sown in the past produced a harvest in your life today that is more abundant than the original investment?

_____
_____
_____
_____

What is the most prominent thing that is happening in your life right now? Can you pinpoint the approximate time when the seeds of thought that gave rise to these events were first planted in your mind?

_____
_____
_____
_____

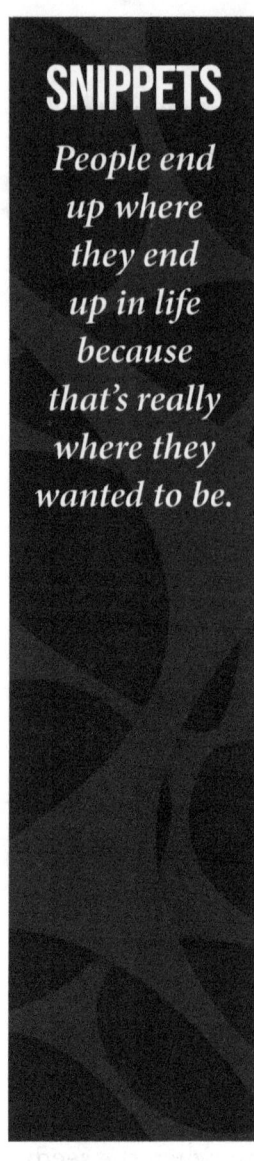

SNIPPETS

People end up where they end up in life because that's really where they wanted to be.

THE FINAL WORD

The significant problems we face in life cannot be solved at the same level of thinking we were at when we created them.
—ALBERT EINSTEIN

Have you ever noticed that whenever there is a problem anywhere in the government, government leaders usually refer the problem back to the same people who created the problem in the first place with a directive for them to solve the problem they created? Perhaps this is why government is so inefficient and why the various departments of government receive consistently low approval ratings from the general public.

The fact of the matter is that no person can solve a problem with the same kind of thinking that gave rise to the problem. If there are things in your life, therefore, that are displeasing to you and unfruitful, you need to do something different. But you cannot do anything different until you start thinking differently about the problem. Until you can approach the unfulfilling parts of your life from a new perspective and with a new attitude, you will just keep doing what you are already doing by force of habit, and tomorrow will look exactly like today (with more wrinkles and gray hair).

Your thoughts are not idle things. Your thoughts matter, because the things you think about, you act upon. And the things you do to act upon your thoughts are the actions that will shape your life and define your character. They will become embedded in your life, and they will eventually determine your destiny and your legacy.

So turn your ship around. In those areas where you know you are headed in a tragic direction, reverse course and start traveling a new path by thinking new thoughts about your life and your deepest ambitions.

PERSONAL JOURNAL

Take a few moments to record your thoughts regarding this week's session on how thoughts become reality. What new things have you learned? What new insights have you received? What life-changing truths did Dr. Dave impart that have impacted you in a meaningful way?

_____
_____
_____
_____
_____
_____
_____
_____
_____
_____
_____
_____
_____
_____
_____
_____
_____
_____
_____
_____
_____
_____
_____
_____

MODULE 5

WHY DON'T PEOPLE KNOW ABOUT THIS?

All of the world's great religions and all of history's leading philosophers have espoused a connection between a person's thinking and the outcome of that person's life. Yet few people ever think about this connection as they plot the course of their lives.

Please refer to Chapter 5 in Dr. Dave Martin's book, *Mindset Matters: Change Your Mind, Change Your World.*

Do you believe that you hold the keys to your own destiny, or do you believe that circumstances and other people determine the course of your life? Explain.

_____
_____
_____
_____
_____
_____

When both religion and philosophy connect our thinking with our behaviors and our behaviors with the quality of our lives, why in your opinion do so many people seem oblivious to this connection?

_____
_____
_____
_____
_____
_____

What do you think Jesus meant when he said, "It shall be done for you as you have believed?"

_____
_____
_____
_____
_____
_____

What does it take to temporarily and artificially override the law of gravity? What are the consequences of trying to override the natural law that connects a person's thinking with his or her destiny in life?

_____
_____
_____
_____

Jesus had to explain to his followers how their beliefs could shape their lives, because these people had never entertained such a concept. How could you best explain this concept to your friends and family members?

_____
_____
_____
_____

Dave Martin proposes that the biggest difference between the four percent who achieve their goals and the ninety-six percent who fail to achieve their goals is the inability of the ninety-six percent to understand the connection between their own thinking and the behaviors that flow from that thinking. In your opinion, to what do these uninformed people attribute the outcomes of their lives?

_____
_____
_____
_____

> ## NUGGETS OF KNOWLEDGE
> *The empires of the future are the empires of the mind.*
> —Winston Churchill
>
> *The future you see is the future you get.*
> —Robert G. Allen

If insanity is doing the same thing over and over while expecting the outcome of that behavior to suddenly change for no reason, why do you think people fail to consider the fact that they must think differently than others if they want to live lives that are different from the people around them?

_____
_____
_____
_____
_____
_____
_____

According to Dave Martin, failure is the "default position in life." Failure is "the default setting for those who do not know what they are doing." What do you think Dr. Dave means by these statements?

_____
_____
_____
_____
_____
_____
_____

According to Dr. Dave, a person will never be able to take full advantage of a truth if that person does not know that the truth exists or if he is unable to apply that truth to his life. What is the truth that most people are missing that can dramatically change both the quality and the direction of their lives?

_____
_____
_____
_____
_____
_____

Most people seem to just float through life like a leaf in the wind or a cork on the open seas. Why, then, do most people expect to arrive at a glorious destination?

_____
_____
_____
_____
_____
_____

SUMMING UP

- Even though some of us may have been surprises for our parents, we were not surprises to God.
- You came from somewhere, and you are definitely traveling somewhere. Your life has meaning.
- Failure is the default position in life. It is the default setting for those who do not know what they are doing.

HANDS ON

There are three important truths that a person must consider as he tries to think about the things that can positively impact his life, that a person must contemplate as she tries to nurture the kind of mindset that will take her to the places she wants to go.

First, there are certain fixed laws in God's creation, laws like gravity and harvesting. What is the primary law, in your opinion, that governs the direction and outcome of a person's life?

_____
_____
_____
_____
_____

Second, each individual has the ability to determine how God's fixed laws will apply to his or her life. How have you determined—consciously or subconsciously—the course of your own life thus far?

_____
_____
_____
_____
_____

Third, most people simply do not know that their own thoughts shape their lives. How can a person come to understand this vital component of his or her success?

_____
_____
_____
_____
_____

SNIPPETS

A man becomes what he does, and a man does what he imagines.

THE FINAL WORD

Nothing in the world is more dangerous than sincere ignorance and conscientious stupidity.
—Martin Luther King, Jr.

What you don't know can definitely hurt you. And this is never truer than when it comes to a person's approach to life. To approach life as if everything will simply fall into place is the height of ignorance, and to expect from life all the benefits that life affords without doing the things that life requires is utter stupidity.

Too many people wait for life to just "happen" for them, hoping that everything will somehow work itself out to their benefit, and feeling utterly shocked when things don't go their way. But even a casual study of theology or philosophy or even a superficial observation of the people around you will tell you that certain people succeed while the majority fail. Logic, therefore, demands that we recognize certain exceptional behaviors that can cause us to triumph over life and certain common behaviors that can cause us to fail.

If you aspire to greatness and to success (whatever that means to you), you must understand that there is a connection between everything in your life. What you do affects what you become, and what you decide affects where you end up. So understand the connection between today's actions and tomorrow's results and between today's choices and tomorrow's consequences because ignorance of these things will not guarantee bliss. Ignorance of these things will only guarantee regret.

PERSONAL JOURNAL

Take a few moments to record your thoughts regarding this week's session on why people do not know that their thoughts shape their lives. What new things have you learned? What new insights have you received? What life-changing truths did Dr. Dave impart that have impacted you in a meaningful way?

_____
_____
_____
_____
_____
_____
_____
_____
_____
_____
_____
_____
_____
_____
_____
_____
_____
_____
_____
_____
_____
_____
_____
_____
_____
_____
_____

MODULE 6

THE PRICE OF SUCCESS

In the same way that nothing moves forward in the physical world without effort and the expenditure of energy, so nothing moves forward in life without effort and the expenditure of energy. There are certain things a person must do to succeed, and those things flow from his or her thinking.

Please refer to Chapter 6 in Dr. Dave Martin's book,
Mindset Matters: Change Your Mind, Change Your World.

What do you think Jesus meant when He told His followers, "Don't begin until you count the cost?"

_____
_____
_____
_____
_____

Give an example of some "good stuff" you have sown into your own mind that is now producing positive results in your life. Give an example of some "bad stuff" that is now producing negative results in your life.

_____
_____
_____
_____
_____

Describe an area of your life where you have discovered your own narrow-mindedness. When you discovered this fault in your thinking, what did you do about it?

_____
_____
_____
_____
_____

According to Dave Martin, we do most of the things that we do in life "by faith." In other words, we do those things without any guarantees, expecting a positive return on our investment in them. Name something important in your life that you have done "by faith."

_____
_____
_____
_____
_____

Are you typically a positive thinker or a negative thinker? Do you expect rain or sunshine? Are you surprised when good things happen for you, or do you usually anticipate good things happening in your life?

_____
_____
_____
_____
_____

Successful people make sacrifices today in order to reap the benefits tomorrow. They say "no" to their appetites today with the expectation of feasting tomorrow on the bounty they produce. Describe a sacrifice you have made in your life that has resulted in measurable benefits.

_____
_____
_____
_____
_____
_____
_____

NUGGETS OF KNOWLEDGE

Some people succeed because they are destined to, but most people succeed because they are determined to.

—Henry Ford

Success is a journey and a destination.

—Tom Denham

The road to success is dotted with many tempting parking spaces.

—Will Rogers

Describe something significant you have achieved in your life by wisely utilizing your spare time. Do you consider yourself a good steward of your spare time?

_____
_____
_____
_____
_____
_____
_____

Do you spend most of your time with people who make you feel comfortable, or do you spend the majority of your time with people who "stretch" you and make you a better person? Why?

_____
_____
_____
_____
_____
_____
_____

Describe an opportunity that you recognized and embraced to the benefit of your own life and destiny. Describe an opportunity that you missed or failed to recognize at the time.

_____
_____
_____
_____
_____

Name a "smart" kid who attended school with you and who failed to live up to people's expectations (first name only). Name a talented student who attended school with you and who failed to live up to people's expectations (first name only). Now name a student who surprised everyone with his or her success in life. What do these real-life observations tell you about success?

_____
_____
_____
_____
_____
_____

SUMMING UP

- If we were all truly unique in our thinking, ninety-six percent of us wouldn't end up in the same wretched place.

- There is no such thing as a problem without a solution.

- Great people make good use of their time, just as they make good use of their money. They don't waste the most precious resources God has entrusted to them.

HANDS ON

There are various components that contribute to a person's success in life. Vision lies at the heart of this "formula," but vision alone cannot guarantee success. Even when a strong vision consumes a person's heart, it is possible for that vision to wane if the vision is not nurtured, so it can grow. The elements that give life to a vision are faith in one's ability to achieve it and a willingness to do whatever is necessary to give that vision life.

What do you "visualize" in your heart and mind whenever you think about your future and the ultimate purpose for your life?

_____
_____
_____
_____
_____

Do you believe you can achieve your dream? Why or why not?

_____
_____
_____
_____
_____

What are some things you believe you will have to do to make your vision a reality? What is the price you will be forced to pay in order to achieve it?

_____
_____
_____
_____
_____

SNIPPETS

Success never comes cheap. It isn't guaranteed to the one who is unwilling to do what it takes to attain it.

THE FINAL WORD

Only those who dare to fail greatly can ever achieve greatly.
—Robert F. Kennedy

One of the greatest impediments to success is the fear of failure. All of us know from our own experiences that it is easier to plan for success and to talk about success than it is to actually take a step toward the things we dream of doing. But it is easier to talk than to do, and it is easier to plan than to execute because all of us fear the self-loathing that can sometimes follow a failure, and we fear the rejection of others perhaps even more.

But even a casual survey of history demonstrates that most of the world's greatest achievers have multiple failures attached to their names. The world's greatest leaders, entrepreneurs, and innovators have suffered setbacks on their journey to the top. Abraham Lincoln, for example, lost several elections before finally becoming president. So the key to overcoming the fear of failure is to look at failure through a different lens. Instead of thinking of failure as the end of it all, we should start thinking of failure as a stepping-stone to victory or a temporary detour on the pathway to greatness.

The story of the world's greatest achievers is a story marked with setbacks and defeats, losses and delays. But setbacks always separate the men from the boys, and grace in the face of defeat always distinguishes the "greats" from the wannabes. So don't despise your failures. Instead, let them become the catalysts that can propel you to greater heights.

PERSONAL JOURNAL

Take a few moments to record your thoughts regarding this week's session on the price of success. What new things have you learned? What new insights have you received? What life-changing truths did Dr. Dave impart that have impacted you in a meaningful way?

MODULE 7

THE PROOF IS IN THE PUDDING

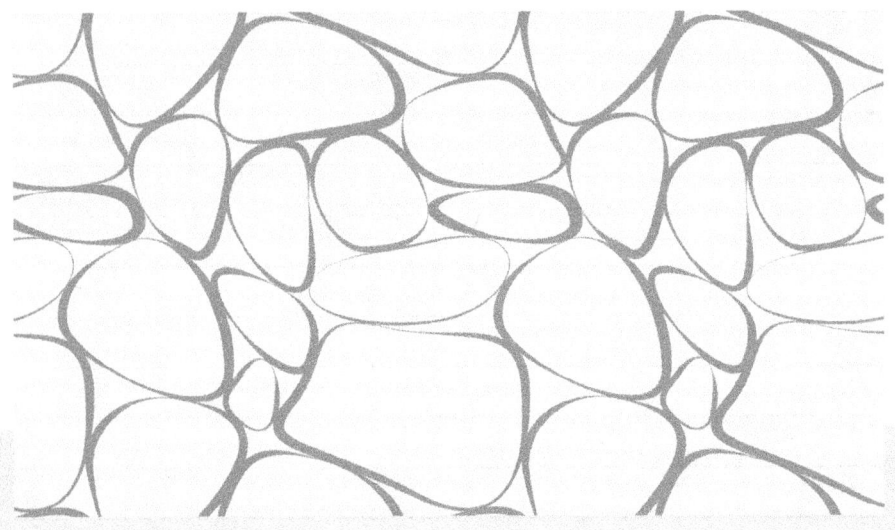

In the same way that only four percent succeed while ninety-six percent fail, most people who read books will never derive the full benefit of the books they read because they will fail to apply the knowledge they have gained. It is important to put newfound knowledge to work as soon as you obtain it, so you can determine whether that knowledge works for you in the real world.

Please refer to Chapter 7 in Dr. Dave Martin's book, *Mindset Matters: Change Your Mind, Change Your World.*

When you read a book, do you tend to put that newly acquired information to work for you, or do you tend to file that information away in the appropriate mental compartment?

_____
_____
_____
_____

What is the primary driving motivation in your life, the one goal that means more to you than anything else? Write it down.

_____
_____
_____
_____

When do you intend to conduct your own personal test of the material in *Mindset Matters: Change Your Mind, Change Your World*? Record the dates.

_____
_____
_____
_____
_____

What do you think Moses meant when he told the Jewish people to impress the laws of God on their children? To talk about them when they sat at home and when they walked along the road, when they went to bed at night and when they got up in the morning? To tie them as symbols on their hands and bind them on their foreheads? To write them on the doorframes of their houses and on their gates?

_____
_____
_____
_____

The test recommended by Dave Martin is designed to help you divert your thoughts from the fears that haunt you and the negative thinking that consumes you and to redirect your thoughts toward a lofty goal that can change the course of your life. What fears do you want to see this test eradicate? What negative thoughts do you want to put behind you?

_____
_____
_____
_____

What is the most ingrained process of thought that you want to eliminate from your life? Can you pinpoint a season in your life when the seeds of thought for this negative perspective began to take root in your life?

_____
_____
_____
_____

> ## NUGGETS OF KNOWLEDGE
>
> *Keep a good attitude and do the right thing even when it's hard. When you do that, you are passing the test.*
> —Joel Osteen
>
> *Here is the test to find whether your mission on earth is finished: if you're alive, it isn't.*
> —Richard Bach
>
> *The greatest barrier to success is the fear of failure.*
> —Sven Goran Erikkson

How do you intend to deal with the ongoing responsibilities of life during your test? How do you plan to deal with the bills, the emergencies, and the other distractions that can easily pull your thoughts back into the gutter of mediocrity?

_____
_____
_____
_____
_____
_____

How will you know when you have achieved success in your life?

_____
_____
_____
_____
_____
_____

Do you believe you have started your own personal journey to success, or have you still found yourself at the starting line, waiting to run the race? Where are you on the journey to success?

_____
_____
_____
_____
_____
_____

How can you inspire yourself as you start this journey? Do you have the purpose you need to succeed? Do you have the faith in yourself that is necessary to complete the effort?

_____
_____
_____
_____
_____
_____

SUMMING UP

- I want you to carry your little card with you everywhere you go, and I want you to look at it several times a day.

- You're never too old to learn something new.

- Your journey to success will never have an actual conclusion because the journey will be ongoing, ever developing, and perpetually evolving into newer and better opportunities.

HANDS ON

If you plan to participate in the test that Dave Martin is recommending as a starting point for transforming your thinking, you will need to identify the driving motivation of your life. Then you will need to expose yourself to that driving motivation throughout the day, so it becomes a central part of your core thinking.

Each morning, when you wake up, you should begin your day by reintroducing yourself to your driving motivation. What are some simple steps you can take in the morning to imbed this vital thinking in your subconscious mind?

_____
_____
_____
_____

Give some examples of things you can do throughout the day to bring your mind back to the driving motivation that is written on your index card.

_____
_____
_____
_____

What can you do at night, just before bedtime, to solidify and strengthen in your mind the things that you need to think about in order to achieve your life's goals?

_____
_____
_____
_____

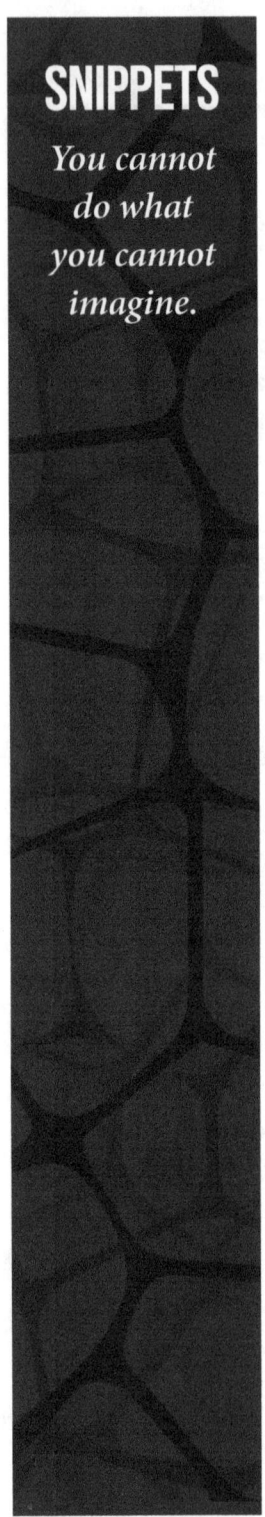

SNIPPETS

You cannot do what you cannot imagine.

THE FINAL WORD

If you want to succeed, you should strike out on new paths rather than travel the worn paths of accepted success.
—JOHN D. ROCKEFELLER

Years ago, Alka-Seltzer ran a series of popular television commercials, featuring characters who would lure their victims into trying a spicy meatball or some other culinary delight by saying, "Try it; you'll like it." But after eating the strange, new food, the victim would always be ready for Alka-Seltzer's fast relief.

Trying new things is always a little dangerous; that's why people don't usually try things that are unfamiliar to them. But the problem with avoiding new experiences is that you can miss out on some of the most wonderful things in life, things that you just might love, things that just might change your life.

You met your husband or wife because you dared to venture into a new circle of friends or into a new place you had never been before. You discovered your favorite restaurant because you once dared to enter that eatery to see if the food was any good. You stumbled across your favorite hobby when someone convinced you to simply try it because you might end up liking it.

We want to challenge you to try the things you have learned in this book. Unlike some publishers, who simply offer you information and then leave you on your own, we want to actually help you change your life. So give our little test a try. What do you have to lose? If the test works for you, your life will be better. If the test doesn't work for you, there's always Alka-Seltzer.

PERSONAL JOURNAL

Take a few moments to record your thoughts regarding this week's session on the test associated with renewed thinking. What new things have you learned? What new insights have you received? What life-changing truths did Dr. Dave impart that have impacted you in a meaningful way?

MODULE 8

YOUR HIGHEST POTENTIAL

When you boil life down to its simplest ingredients, success is not an accident. Success is the product of one's accumulative actions, and actions are the product of one's accumulative thoughts.

Please refer to Chapter 8 in Dr. Dave Martin's book,
Mindset Matters: Change Your Mind, Change Your World.

The vast majority of the things that happen to us are the direct result of choices we have made, actions we have taken, words we have uttered, or attitudes we have exhibited. Give an example from your own life of something that is happening to you right now as a result of your past actions or decisions.

_____
_____
_____
_____
_____
_____

Nobody can achieve anything meaningful without paying a price. What is the most meaningful thing you have achieved in your life thus far? What is the price you were required to pay for that achievement?

_____
_____
_____
_____
_____
_____
_____
_____

Success is in direct proportion to the effort a person puts forth to achieve it and the price he has paid to obtain it. Give an example of the price somebody has paid to do something meaningful with his or her life.

_____
_____
_____
_____
_____

Give an example of some "seeds" you have planted in the past that are yielding an unwanted harvest in your life right now. What new "seeds" can you start sowing today to produce a different harvest in the future?

_____
_____
_____
_____
_____

Can you name someone who grew up in your hometown and then moved away to a different state or a different country? How did this move affect his or her thinking? How did this move affect the outcome of that person's life?

_____
_____
_____
_____
_____

NUGGETS OF KNOWLEDGE

The individual has always had to struggle to keep from being overwhelmed by the tribe. If you try it, you will be lonely often, and sometimes frightened. But no price is too high to pay for the privilege of owning yourself.
—Friedrich Nietzsche

The price of greatness is responsibility.
—Winston Churchill

If you believe in yourself and have dedication and pride and never quit, you'll be a winner. The price of victory is high, but so are the rewards.
—Paul Bryant

The person who stays trapped in his own limited thinking is the person who is incapable of seeing what is beyond the horizon. Describe something that is present in your life today that you were unable to visualize or imagine in the past. How has this experience changed the way you think?

_____
_____
_____
_____
_____

What do you think Dave Ramsey means when he says, "If you will live like no one else, later you can live like no one else"?

_____
_____
_____
_____
_____

Most people who fall in the ninety-six percent are people who try to live a sultan's lifestyle the day they leave their parents' home. When you first moved out on your own, did you fall into the trap of trying to maintain your parents' lifestyle, or did you learn early the virtues of living beneath your means and saving your money? What happened as a result of your early choices?

_____
_____
_____
_____
_____

What do you think Albert Einstein meant when he said, "Compound interest is the eighth wonder of the world"?

_____
_____
_____
_____
_____

What "baby steps" can you take right now to start thinking and acting like the four percent who succeed in life?

_____
_____
_____
_____
_____
_____
_____

SUMMING UP

- The vast majority of the things that happen to us are things that result from the choices we have made, the actions we have taken, the words we have uttered, or the attitudes we have exhibited.

- Your life is the product of your own actions. You are where you are today because you did things in the past to place yourself there.

- Most people who fall into the ninety-six percent are people who try to live a sultan's lifestyle the day they leave their parents' home.

HANDS ON

Each person's definition of success is different because each person's vision for his life is different. But the common thread that runs through every pursuit of a dream is the thread of sacrifice that a person must be willing to make in order to achieve the dream within one's heart.

For one thing, a person must be willing to control his or her thoughts if that person intends to control his or her life. What thoughts do you need to nurture in your life if you intend to fulfill the things that lie buried within your heart?

_____
_____
_____
_____
_____
_____
_____

A person must also be willing to remove all fetters from his mind and allow his mind to soar if that person hopes to achieve his highest potential in life. What self-imposed limitations do you need to remove from your thought processes before you can hope to do great things?

_____
_____
_____
_____
_____
_____
_____

In order to succeed, a person must be willing to discipline himself to think positively about himself and about life. How have you sabotaged your own best efforts in the past through negative thinking about yourself or your potential?

_____
_____
_____
_____
_____
_____
_____
_____

To achieve her dreams and goals, a person must be willing to live like nobody else, so she can eventually live like nobody else. What financial sacrifices do you know you will have to make in order to get where you want to be? How will that sacrifice be worth the price when you finally arrive at your destination?

_____
_____
_____
_____
_____
_____
_____
_____
_____

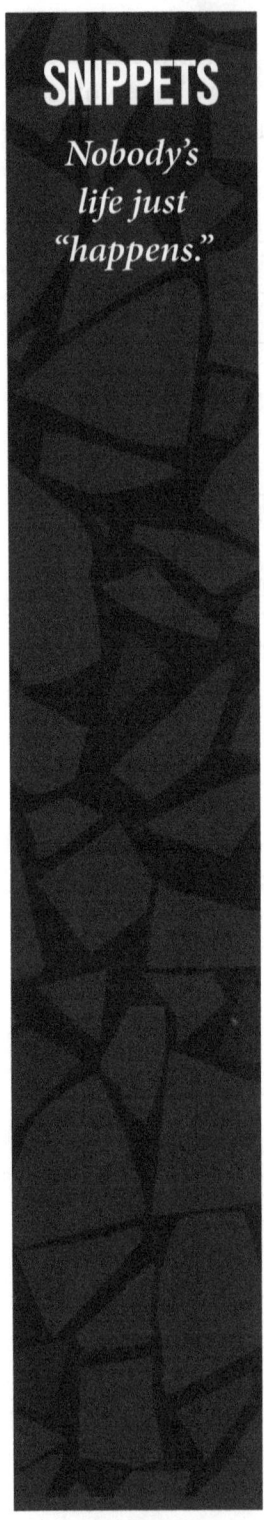

SNIPPETS

Nobody's life just "happens."

THE FINAL WORD

When you want something you've never had, you have to do something you've never done.
—THOMAS JEFFERSON

Over the course of this study, we have explored many dynamics that separate the successful from the unsuccessful. We have explored many qualities that distinguish the "greats" from the wannabes. In the end, however, greatness and success come down to achievement, and achievement comes down to one's thinking. So in the end, those who are unsuccessful in their lives must determine to do something different in order to make the rest of their lives the best of their lives.

Just think about this for a moment! If you continue doing the same things tomorrow that you are doing today, you really won't have a tomorrow. Instead, you will just have a longer "today." When a person can hope for nothing more tomorrow than a repeat of today's activities and achievements, there really is no promise of a brighter future, only a promise of an extended day.

To make tomorrow better than today, therefore, one simple and logical rule must preside: You must do something different. If you want to be something you have never been, go places you have never gone, achieve things you have never achieved, or produce something you have never produced, you will have to do something different from this point forward than you have been doing in the past. Change is the essence of success, and all change begins with a changed mind.

PERSONAL JOURNAL

Take a few moments to record your thoughts regarding this week's session on the price of success. What new things have you learned? What new insights have you received? What life-changing truths did Dr. Dave impart that have impacted you in a meaningful way?

www.ingramcontent.com/pod-product-compliance
Lightning Source LLC
Chambersburg PA
CBHW062120080426
42734CB00012B/2934